Series 999

The Ladybird Grown–Up Picture Books are ideally suited for use with the Ladybird 'Over The Hill' series.

A LADYBIRD

First Grown–Up Picture Book

by J.A. HAZELEY, N.S.F.W.
and J.P. MORRIS, O.M.G.

(Authors of 'What To Look For In The Worst Case Scenario')

Publishers: Ladybird Books Ltd., Loughborough
Printed in England. If wet, Italy.

work

Talking about going to work:

Why are there no trains again?
What does "passenger action" mean?
Will I ever get to work? Why is it taking so long to
get somewhere that I do not even want to be?
Can I retrain as a contract killer?

cholesterol

Talking about cholesterol:

How can I reduce my cholesterol if I don't understand what it is?
Isn't it butter? Less butter, more fruit. Is that the general idea? So this fruit pie is fine as long as I don't spread any butter on it, right?

insurance

Talking about insurance:

Why do I spend so much on insurance?
Isn't it just gambling? But more boring?
If I threw away this much on scratchcards or the
horses, wouldn't I think I had a problem?
With the money I spend on all these premiums
couldn't I buy something that made me happier?
Then why don't I?

stationery

Talking about stationery:

Why don't any of these flaming pens work?
Who keeps putting pens that don't work back in
this drawer? What is wrong with some people?
We're always buying pens. Where on earth do
they go? Are all the socks there too?

farmer's market

Talking about the farmer's market:

How much are these carrots?
What, per kilogram?
Each? Really? What does "heritage" mean?
Could I just have an onion, then, please?
Oh. Do you take credit cards?

columnists

Talking about columnists:

Why did someone write this rubbish?
How can they get away with it?
Did they know I'd get angry? Was that the idea? To
provoke a reaction, to make me angry?
Why does that make me so angry?

running

Talking about running:

Why am I running? Where am I going?
Do I want a longer life if I have to spend so much of it running?
Why aren't I at home? Am I running away from home? Am I scared of home? Why is my brain full of weird, horrible thoughts? Is it because running is so very, very boring?
Why did I forget my headphones?

passive aggression

Talking about passive aggression:

No, it's OK, I'll answer it.
Yes, I know you're busy, but the thing is — you're busy near the front door. I'm not.
Clearly you think this decking will lay itself.
Yes. What is it?
Well, if he really loved me, Jesus would let me get on with this decking, wouldn't he?

wine

Talking about wine:

It's 3pm. Is that too early? How early is too early? How come when we go round to their place, we take a nice £13 bottle, and when they come to ours, they bring some muck worth about a fiver? Who cares if it's corked? It's still wine.

landfill

Talking about landfill:

Who left this here where I could tread on it?
Where did it come from? A party bag? A comic? A
happy meal?
How do the kids acquire so much plastic toot?
If I throw this in the bin, just to clear some space,
they'll know, won't they?
How? How do they know?

estate agents

Talking about estate agents:

What did the entire human race do in another life
to deserve estate agents?
Is there something like garlic or sunlight or silver
that keeps them at bay?
Is it legal to hunt them?

hip-hop

Talking about hip-hop:

Listen to the way the beat drops. Can you hear it?
Say these words: shizzle, bizzle, for rizzle.
Is this old skool hip-hop? But it only came out ten
years ago.
Skepta. I've heard of them. Are they hip-hop?

28

vasectomy

Talking about vasectomy:

Should I buy one of those inflatable cushions?
How often does the operation go wrong?
Will it still, you know, "work"?
I won't get a high voice or moobs, will I?
Do I get 14 days to change my mind afterwards?

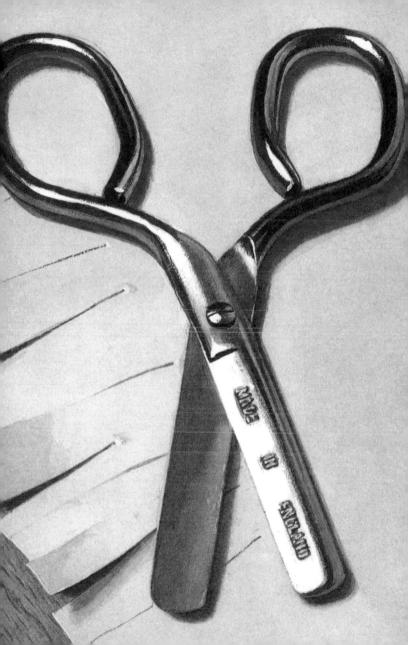

dieting

Talking about dieting:

If I'm only allowed a single egg for lunch, why can't it be this big?
Are they absolutely sure toast is off–limits?
Do I feel healthier? Or just hungrier and unhappier?
Hang on — wasn't Atkins killed by his own diet?

my face

Talking about my face:

Is that really my face?
Who put all those lines on it?
When did I start to look like W.H. Auden?

back–ache

Talking about back–ache:

Why does it hurt when I stand up?
What is in these tablets? Why is it not working?
Can I mix these with the ones left over from the
vasectomy?
Does gin count as a muscle relaxant?

holiday

Talking about going on holiday:

Are we there yet?
Are we there yet?
Are we there yet?
Are we there yet?
Are we there yet?

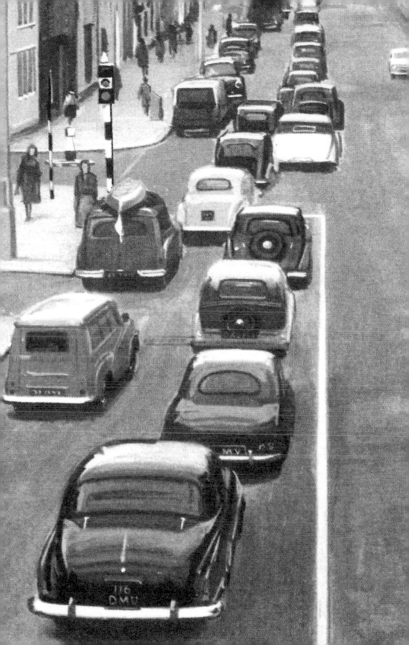

birthdays

Talking about birthdays:

I can't be that old, can I?
If I don't tell anyone it's my birthday, and don't
mind not getting any presents, can I stay the same
age for another year?
Can I speak to someone in charge about this?

menopause

Talking about the menopause:

Ten minutes ago I felt fine. So why do I now feel
like I'm on holiday in a rice steamer?
Everything seems to be permanently ON.
Hang on. It's all gone off.
Well, this is a right OH WAIT IT'S ALL ON AGAIN.

hair loss

Talking about losing your hair:

Does it look like a full head of hair if I do this?
How about this?
Should I just shave it all off?
Will that make me look like a potato?
Would those clinics be allowed to advertise if it
didn't work? Do we really need a holiday this year?

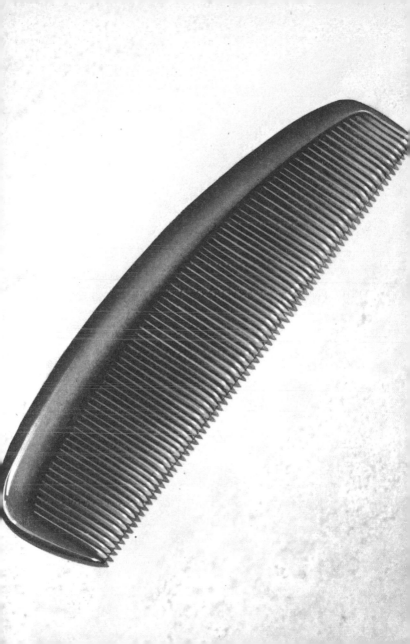

nostalgia

Talking about nostalgia:

Wasn't everything better in the old days?
Except polio. Oh, and skinheads. And acid rain.
And quicksand. And rabies. And that flesh—eating
disease. And conscription. And bad sausages.
Still, at least everything was cheaper.

lost

Talking about feeling lost:

What on earth am I doing here?
Why did I agree to pay £200 for my daughter to
watch a spotty YouTuber with amazing hair and
bad diction open some boxes live on stage?
How many kids must be here? 70,000? More?
Is this the most out–of–touch I have ever felt?

insignificance

Talking about insignificance:

What am I here for?
What does any of it matter?
What if I die tomorrow?
What if nobody tends my grave and the plot is given to someone else? What if I leave nothing behind to show I was ever here?
Ooh. Have I seen this episode of Storage Hunters?

obsolete

Talking about obsolescence:

Why have I still got this old thing?
Did I keep it just in case? Just in case of what?
Don't I have something on my phone that does this? But better?
Why can't I bring myself to get rid of this? Is it because if the camera is obsolete, so am I?

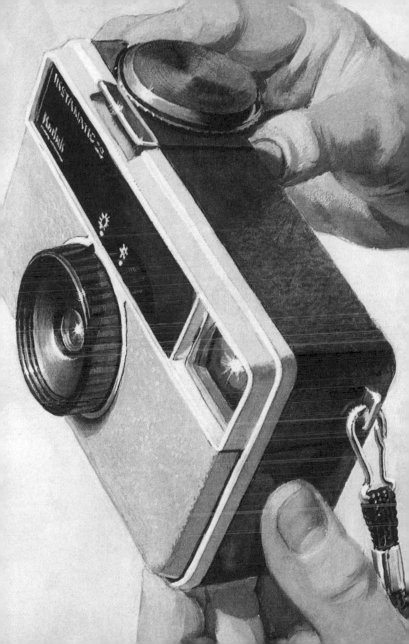

THE AUTHORS would like to record their gratitude and offer their apologies to the many Ladybird artists whose luminous work formed the glorious wallpaper of countless childhoods. Revisiting it for this book as grown-ups has been a privilege.

MICHAEL JOSEPH

UK | USA | Canada | Ireland | Australia
India | New Zealand | South Africa

Michael Joseph is part of the Penguin Random House group of companies whose addresses can be found at global.penguinrandomhouse.com

First published 2017
001

Printed in Italy by L.E.G.O. S.p.A

A CIP catalogue record for this book is available from the British Library

ISBN: 978–0–718–18884–9

www.greenpenguin.co.uk

MIX
Paper from
responsible sources
FSC® C018179

Penguin Random House is committed to a sustainable future for our business, our readers and our planet. This book is made from Forest Stewardship Council® certified paper.